I KNOW AMERICA

Our
Congress

Michael Weber

THE MILLBROOK PRESS
Brookfield, Connecticut

Published by The Millbrook Press
2 Old New Milford Road
Brookfield, CT 06804

10 9 8 7 6 5 4 3 2 1

Created and produced in association with Blackbirch Graphics.
Series Editor: Tanya Lee Stone

Library of Congress Cataloging-in-Publication Data
Weber, Michael (Michael L.)
    Our Congress / Michael Weber.
        p.   cm. — (I know America)
    Includes bibliographical references and index.
    Summary: Describes Congress's role as one of the three main branches of
our government.
    ISBN 1-56294-443-6
    1. United States—Congress—Juvenile literature. [1. United States—
Congress] I. Title. II. Series.
JK1061.W45   1994
328.73'07—dc20   94-7639
                                                                    CIP
                                                                    AC

Acknowledgments and Photo Credits
Cover: National Park Service/U.S. Department of Interior; pp. 5,18, 22, 32,
34, 38, 40, 42, 43: Wide World Photos, Inc.; pp. 6, 9, 10, 11, 12, 13, 19,
24, 28: ©Blackbirch Press, Inc.; p. 14: North Wind Picture Archives; pp.16,
30: ©Terry Ashe/Gamma Liaison; pp. 21, 26, 27: ©Brad Markel/Gamma
Liaison.

CONTENTS

The large, white dome of the Capitol building in Washington, D.C., has long been a powerful symbol of our nation's government. Inside that building, the most important decisions about our country are made.

The Capitol building is home to the legislative (lawmaking) branch of the U.S. government, also known as Congress. Congress is the most powerful lawmaking body in the land. Along with the president of the United States, Congress creates and passes laws that govern the lives of all Americans. For example, Congress decides how much each citizen must pay in federal taxes. It also decides how the government will spend all the money it takes in from taxpayers. And Congress passes laws that protect civil rights and help the needy. Congress can even declare war and propose amendments that change the Constitution. The Constitution is the document that contains the basic laws upon which our country was founded.

Congress is actually made up of two houses, or governing bodies: the House of Representatives and the Senate. The House of Representatives is made up of 435 Congressmen and Congresswomen from every

state in America. The Senate is made up of 100 senators—two from each state. The House and the Senate must work closely together to write, amend, and pass laws.

Every November in even-numbered years, the American people vote to elect, or re-elect, members of Congress. This new Congress meets the following January in the Capitol building and works for two years until new elections change Congress's makeup once again.

In the pages that follow, you will read more about the powers of the House and Senate and learn more about how Congress works.

One month after their election to the 103d Congress, new senators and representatives pose for a photo outside the Capitol building in December 1992.

THE BEGINNING

The U.S. Congress was created more than two hundred years ago, when America was still very young. Political leaders and statesmen from the thirteen colonies debated and argued for months about how Congress and the federal government should be organized. These people, known as our country's Founding Fathers, worked hard to develop a system of government that would represent all of America's citizens. Their hopes and desires were to create a new, more democratic government.

The Colonial Background

When colonists first came to America from England in the 1600s, they were loyal to the king of England and believed they possessed the same rights as the people still living in England.

Opposite: **Alexander Hamilton participated in the Constitutional Convention. There, he helped plan our Constitution, which is the foundation of our government.**

For example, the colonists expected to be able to elect local representatives who would govern them. They also believed they would not be taxed without their agreement, and they thought they would be in control of how their government spent their money.

In each of the thirteen colonies, there was an elected assembly, or legislature. Each colony also had a governor.

Back in England, the lawmaking part of the government was called Parliament, which is still in existence today. The colonists, unlike people living in England, had no part in choosing any of the members of Parliament.

From 1754 to 1763, Britain fought a war with France that extended to many parts of the world. In North America, the war was called the French and Indian War. Britain sent troops to America to fight against the French and several Indian tribes who were France's allies.

Britain won, but the war had been very expensive. The king and Parliament began to look at the American colonies as a source of income. They wanted the colonists to pay more taxes. They also wanted to maintain an army of soldiers in America, which the colonists would have to house and support. The British government even prevented American merchants from trading in markets where British merchants also traded.

As the British placed more taxes and regulations on America, the colonists protested. In 1773, outraged colonists threw tons of British tea into Boston Harbor to protest laws that discriminated against American tea merchants. This protest was known as the Boston Tea Party.

In 1773, angry colonists destroyed crates of British tea to protest new taxes and laws imposed on them by the British.

The Continental Congresses

Colonial leaders of the protests against Britain decided that delegates from all of the colonies should meet and develop a plan of action against the British.

This meeting, the First Continental Congress, was held in Philadelphia during September and October 1774. Twelve of the thirteen colonies were represented. Only Georgia failed to send anyone. Each colony had one vote in the Congress.

The Congress adopted a declaration stating that many laws passed by Parliament since 1763 violated the rights of the American colonists. The Congress also called on Americans not to buy any British goods until those laws were repealed. It provided for a second Congress to meet in May 1775 if Britain had not met its demands by then.

Most American leaders wanted the dispute with Britain to be settled peacefully. But by spring of 1775, the situation had turned violent. In April, British and

American soldiers fought battles at Lexington and Concord, two Massachusetts towns. The American Revolution had begun.

The Second Continental Congress began on May 10, 1775, again in Philadelphia. This time, all thirteen colonies were represented.

The Congress organized an army and chose George Washington to command it. While the delegates worked, more battles were taking place. Still, the Congress hoped the differences with Britain could be worked out. But in the fall, Americans learned that King George III had proclaimed the colonies to be in open rebellion.

Now, for the first time, Americans began thinking seriously about independence from Britain. In the spring and summer of 1776, the Congress debated the issue in detail. On July 2, it voted for independence. On July 4, it approved the Declaration of Independence written by Thomas Jefferson. What had formerly been thirteen British colonies were now the thirteen states of the United States of America.

The battle between the British troops (on the left in this engraving) and the American colonists, which took place in the town of Concord, Massachusetts, helped mark the start of the American Revolution.

Congress Under the Articles of Confederation

The new nation now had to fight for its freedom. It also needed a permanent government. In July 1776, a committee of the Second Continental Congress prepared a plan for a government, called the Articles of Confederation and Perpetual Union.

The government created by the Articles of Confederation was a simple one. Basically, it was a continuation of the Second Continental Congress, with each state having one vote.

The Congress was weak. It could not tax people. It could only *ask* the states for money. It could not regulate trade, either among the states or between America and other countries. There was no executive branch of government to enforce the laws and no judicial branch to interpret them. And the Articles could only be amended if all the states agreed.

After 1783, when Britain recognized America's independence, the government's weakness led to serious problems. It could not pay its debts, and the money the government issued declined sharply in value. States quarrelled with each other, and many foreign nations had little respect for the new country.

Several leading Americans—including George Washington, James Madison, and Alexander Hamilton—felt the government had to be strengthened. A new convention was held to consider what to do.

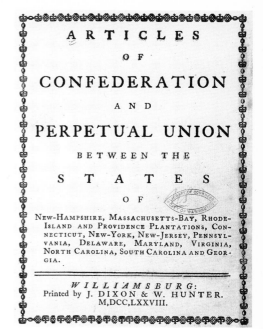

ARTICLES OF CONFEDERATION AND PERPETUAL UNION BETWEEN THE STATES OF

New-Hampshire, Massachusetts-Bay, Rhode-Island and Providence Plantations, Connecticut, New-York, New-Jersey, Pennsylvania, Delaware, Maryland, Virginia, North Carolina, South Carolina and Georgia.

WILLIAMSBURG:
Printed by J. DIXON & W. HUNTER.
M,DCC,LXXVIII.

The cover of the Articles of Confederation and Perpetual Union. This document created a plan for a new government.

11

The Constitutional Convention

The convention met in Philadelphia in 1787, and decided to scrap the Articles of Confederation entirely to create a new government. The delegates wrote the U.S. Constitution, the document that specifies the structure and powers of America's government.

The task of the delegates was a difficult one. They wanted to create a national government for America that could govern effectively. But they wanted to make sure the new government would not interfere with the people's freedom and liberty.

The Constitution created a government with three independent branches. The legislative branch would consist of a new kind of Congress that would make laws and have other important powers. An executive branch, headed by the president, would run the government and enforce the laws. A third branch, the judiciary, would consist of a Supreme Court and any other courts that Congress might create. The judiciary would interpret the laws and punish people who violated them.

Each branch could somewhat influence and control the actions of the other branches. This is called the system of checks and balances. Many actions of the

Delegates to the Constitutional Convention of 1787 created a strong government with three branches.

president, for example, must be approved by a vote in Congress. Similarly, the president has the power to sign or veto legislation that is passed by Congress. But the Founding Fathers expected that Congress would be the most powerful branch.

The Great Compromise

As the delegates worked to write the Constitution, they had many disagreements. At times, it seemed as if the convention might dissolve. The most serious debate concerned representation in the new Congress.

The basic idea for a government composed of different branches had been presented in a plan offered by the delegates from Virginia. Among them was James Madison, who has been called the "father of the Constitution" because he played such a prominent role in writing it.

Under the Virginia Plan, Congress would consist of two houses, or parts. The members of one house would be chosen directly by the people in each state. States with large populations would elect more representatives than states with small populations. The members of the second house of Congress would be chosen by the members of the first house.

Convention delegates from the smaller states vigorously objected to this plan. They feared it would give large states too much power. Instead, they presented the New Jersey Plan. In this plan, Congress would consist of just one house, like the Congress under the Articles of Confederation. In this house,

James Madison supported the idea that members of Congress should be elected by residents of each state of the Union.

One tax imposed by the British that outraged the American colonists was the Stamp Act of 1765. This law required the colonists to purchase stamps for newspapers, pamphlets, leases, and many other common documents—including playing cards. Colonial leaders, such as Patrick Henry of Virginia, claimed this was "taxation without representation." The Massachusetts assembly called for a meeting of delegates from all of the colonies to protest the law. This Stamp Act Congress met in New York City in October 1765, although representatives of only nine of the colonies attended. The Congress issued a statement claiming that the Stamp Act violated the colonists' rights and liberties as Englishmen.

The Congress's Stamp Act protest was effective. Parliament repealed the law in 1766. At the same time, however, it passed another, stating that it had the power to make laws for America "in all cases whatsoever."

The Stamp Act riot in Boston in 1765.

each state would have one vote. Thus, small states would have as much power in Congress as large ones.

The argument between the large states and the small ones was very bitter. Finally, a compromise was worked out. Under it, Congress would have two houses. As in the Virginia Plan, one house, the House of Representatives, would be elected by the people in each state. The number of representatives a state had would be determined by its size. But in the second house, the Senate, each state would have two senators, regardless of its population.

Other difficult issues remained for the Constitutional Convention to settle. But this Great Compromise, as it came to be called, put the convention on the way to a successful conclusion.

Ratification of the Constitution

After the delegates finished writing the Constitution, they submitted it to the states for ratification, or approval. Nine states had to ratify the Constitution for it to take effect.

The ratification process involved lengthy debate. Many people feared that the new government would be too powerful. The most serious objection to the Constitution was that it lacked a Bill of Rights specifically stating what rights the people and the states possess that the national government cannot take away. Not until supporters of the Constitution promised that a Bill of Rights would be added did the required nine states ratify the Constitution.

The new government, with George Washington elected as the first president of the United States, began work in early 1789. The first Congress under the Constitution promptly began work on a Bill of Rights, which became the first ten amendments to the Constitution. The first Congress also created the U.S. Postal Service and the State, Treasury, and War departments of the government, as well as a system of courts. The government we have today had begun.

OUR REPRESENTATIVES AND SENATORS

Drafting the Constitution during the Constitutional Convention of 1787 was a long and complicated process. But the final result was an extraordinary document that provided the basis for the creation of an entire democracy. Today, more than two hundred years after its signing, the Constitution still remains the backbone of our society. Its usefulness over the centuries is proof of its long-lasting power and beauty.

Opposite: Senators Joseph Lieberman (left), Diane Feinstein (middle), and Frank Lautenberg (right), talk before a Congressional debate.

The House of Representatives

The House of Representatives—also referred to simply as the House—consists of 435 representatives, or members of Congress. Each representative has one vote, except in the rare situation when the House has to choose the president. Then the voting is by state.

The Constitution provides that each state has representatives in Congress in proportion to its population. The larger the state's population, the more representatives it has. But every state must have at least one representative.

In the first Congress under the Constitution, there were a total of only 65 representatives. As America's population grew, so did the number of representatives. In 1911, Congress set the maximum at 435 so that the House would not become too large to operate efficiently.

Every ten years, the United States government counts the number of people in the whole country. This count is called the census. Once the number of people in each state is known, the number of representatives each state is entitled to have in

Members of the House are sworn in on January 5, 1993, the first day of the 103d Congress.

CONGRESSIONAL FACTS AND TIDBITS

The face of Congress is constantly changing. In recent years, more women and minorities have been elected by voters, and the average age of senators and representatives has been getting younger. Here are some interesting facts about the makeup of Congress past and present.

• The first woman in Congress was Jeannette Rankin of Montana, elected in 1916.

• The first African American in Congress was Joseph H. Rainey of South Carolina, elected in 1870.

• Members of Congress have come from all walks of life; some have been newspaper publishers, bankers, tax accountants, restaurant owners, real estate brokers, farmers, and social workers. Senator Bill Bradley from New Jersey was a professional basketball star. Senator John Glenn of Ohio orbited the Earth as an astronaut.

• The majority of Congressional members are lawyers.

• In 1993, seventy-seven members of Congress had education or teaching backgrounds.

Jeannette Rankin

• The average age of a U.S. senator in 1993 was fifty-eight.

• The average age of a U.S. representative in 1993 was fifty-one.

• The youngest person in Congress in 1993 was Representative Cleo Fields of Louisiana, who was thirty years old.

• The oldest member of Congress in 1993 was Senator Strom Thurmond of South Carolina, who was ninety-one years old.

• There were forty-eight women in the House of Representatives and seven in the Senate in 1993.

• Altogether, more than 23,000 staff employees work for Congress.

Congress can be determined. The 1990 census determined that California is the largest state in population, so until at least the year 2000 it has the most representatives—fifty-two. New York is second, with thirty-one representatives. Seven states—Alaska, Delaware, Montana, North Dakota, South Dakota, Vermont, and Wyoming—each have only one representative.

The Constitution intended the House of Representatives to be the part of the government that is closest to the people. For this reason, representatives serve short terms and are elected directly by the people. All the representatives come up for re-election every two years. Each representative is elected from a specific district within a state. Each state's legislature decides the boundaries of its districts.

The Constitution requires that each representative be a resident of the state from which he or she is elected. But the representative does not have to live in the district where he or she is elected. A representative must be at least twenty-five years old and must have been a citizen of the United States for at least seven years.

The Senate

The Senate is different from the House in several ways. Unlike the House's representation based on state population, the Senate has two senators from each state. Today, since there are fifty states, the Senate has one hundred members.

Senators serve terms of six years, which is three times as long as representatives. A senator must be at least thirty years old, be a resident of the state where he or she is elected, and have been a citizen of the United States for at least nine years. Unlike in the House of Representatives, only one third of all the senators are up for re-election every two years. The other senators have either two or four more years left in their terms, as established in the Constitution.

Senator John Danforth (speaking) discusses a Congressional plan with the press in June 1992.

The Constitution originally intended the Senate to be a group of wise statesmen who were not directly dependent on the will of the people. For this reason, it provided that senators would serve longer terms than representatives and that they would not be directly elected by the people. Each state's senators were to be chosen by its state legislature. The Constitution also gave the Senate certain powers not shared by the House. We will read about these powers in Chapter 3.

But in 1913, the Seventeenth Amendment to the Constitution was ratified. It changed the method for electing senators, so that they too are now directly elected by the voters in each state. The terms and powers of senators, however, were unchanged by the Seventeenth Amendment.

CONGRESSIONAL LEADERS

The leader of the House of Representatives is called the Speaker of the House. As specified in the Constitution, the Speaker is elected by the House at the beginning of each new Congress and is always a member of the majority party in the House. The Speaker can influence what business comes before the House, who speaks during debates, what work House committees do, who is chosen to serve on committees, and other important matters.

Second in command is the majority leader. The Speaker and the majority leader are assisted by the majority whip and assistant whips who help keep all of the members informed of each others'

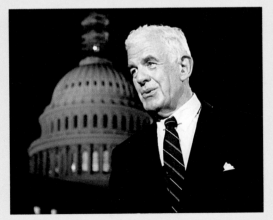

Speaker of the House Thomas Foley talks to reporters at the Capitol building in 1993.

views. And as their name implies, the whips round up members when an important vote is coming up. The minority party in the House also elects a minority leader, a minority whip, and assistant whips. Party leaders and whips are chosen in special closed meetings, called caucuses or conferences. In these meetings, influential and powerful party members negotiate for position and roles within the party.

For the Senate, the Constitution provides that the presiding officer is the vice president of the United States. But the vice president normally cannot vote on issues before the Senate. The only time the vice president can vote is when the Senate's vote is tied.

If the vice president is absent, the Senate is presided over by a senator called the president pro tempore. That is Latin for "temporary president."

But the real leaders of the Senate are the majority and minority leaders and their whips. The majority leader of the Senate has powers similar to those of the Speaker of the House.

Political Parties in Congress

There is one very important aspect of Congress—and of most of the United States government—that is not mentioned at all in the Constitution. That aspect is the role that is played by political parties. Political parties are groups of people organized for the purpose of directing the policies of the government and supporting candidates running for public office. Although the Constitution does not address the issue of political parties, they have been essential to the work of Congress since the 1790s.

The organization of both the Senate and the House of Representatives is based on political parties. For many years, the two main political parties in the United States have been the Democrats and the Republicans. These two major parties have historically dominated Congress.

The majority party in each house of Congress is the one to which more than half the members belong. If fewer than half the members in Congress belong to a certain party, that party is said to be the minority. The majority party can control what business is taken up and debated, when the business is considered, and can usually determine what action is taken.

The Democratic party has been the majority party in Congress for most of the years since 1933 except four: 1947, 1948, 1953, and 1954. They have also been the majority in the Senate for every year since 1933 except 1947–1948, 1953–1954, and 1981–1986.

23

3

THE POWERS OF CONGRESS

The U.S. Congress is the most powerful lawmaking body in America. The laws it passes and the decisions it makes affect nearly all aspects of daily life in our country. It has a direct impact on everything from the crops our farmers grow, to the programs we watch on television, to the way our cars are built. Because it affects so many aspects of society, members of Congress work day and night addressing the biggest issues that face our country today.

Congress Makes Laws

Congress makes the laws that govern America. Through this power, Congress affects the lives of every person in our country. Congress authorizes the government to issue the money that we use every day.

Opposite: **Congress meets in the U.S. Capitol building in Washington, D.C.**

25

It establishes federal taxes and decides how the government spends that money. It also authorizes the government to borrow money.

Congress passes laws that regulate trade among the states, as well as with other nations. It makes the rules by which immigrants can become American citizens. It even defines the weights and measures—pounds and inches, for example—that we use every day. It also writes laws that protect the work of inventors and authors through strict commercial regulations and copyrights.

Congress controls the admission of new states to the United States. It also governs the District of Columbia, which contains the city of Washington, the capital of our nation.

Congress Oversees and Conducts Investigations

Since Congress creates the departments of the government and appropriates, or provides, the money they spend, it also watches over them to see that they do their jobs properly. The General Accounting Office (known as the GAO) and the Congressional Budget Office (CBO) are two agencies created by Congress to help it watch the rest of the government.

Congress can also conduct investigations into a certain foreign policy activity or a domestic issue that is causing concern. A committee may ask people involved to come before it and testify. Sometimes these investigations are broadcast on television.

U.S. Marine Lieutenant Colonel Oliver North responds to a question during congressional hearings in 1987 regarding his involvement with the sale of weapons to Iran.

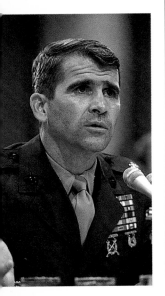

Congress Confirms and Ratifies

One house of Congress—the Senate—has the very important power to confirm presidential appointments and ratify (approve by vote) treaties.

The president nominates, or chooses, people for many important offices. These include the members of the Supreme Court, ambassadors, heads of government departments and agencies, and top military officers. But before these people can take office, the Senate must agree to their appointments by majority vote. If the Senate does not vote to confirm, the president must nominate another person.

The Senate must also ratify all treaties, or agreements, that the president has negotiated with other countries. A treaty must be ratified by a two-thirds majority of the Senate.

Congress Impeaches and Tries Federal Officials

A rarely used power of Congress is the impeachment of federal officials. To impeach a person means to bring charges of serious misconduct against him or her. If the official is then convicted of the charges, he or she is removed from office.

The House of Representatives decides whether to impeach an official. If a majority votes to impeach, the Senate, acting like a court, then tries the official. A two-thirds vote of the Senate is needed to convict the person. Congress has impeached and convicted several federal judges.

Ruth Bader Ginsburg is sworn in as a Supreme Court Justice on August 10, 1993, after having been confirmed by the Senate.

THE IMPEACHMENT OF A PRESIDENT

No president has ever been impeached and convicted, but two have come very close.

Shortly after the Civil War, Congress and President Andrew Johnson sharply disagreed over policies toward the Southern states, the freed slaves, and other issues. Their disputes grew so bitter that in 1868, leaders of Congress tried to use the impeachment process to remove Johnson from office. The

Andrew Johnson's impeachment trial in the Senate chamber.

House voted to impeach him on eleven charges. But the Senate refused to convict him. On one charge, the Senate fell only one vote short of the two-thirds majority needed to convict.

In 1974, President Richard Nixon became the second president to be nearly impeached. As a result of Nixon's role in the Watergate scandal (a scandal that involved both the president and other officials abusing their powers of office), a House committee voted to impeach him on three charges. It seemed certain that the full House would agree and that the Senate would vote to convict. Nixon then decided to resign, becoming the only president to do so.

Congress Declares War

The president is the commander-in-chief of the armed forces that Congress creates. But only Congress can declare war with another nation. The United States, however, has sometimes fought major conflicts, including the Korean and Vietnam wars, without the declaration of war by Congress.

Congress's Other Powers

Congress plays an important role in amending the Constitution. Congress can, if two thirds of each house agrees, propose amendments. Alternatively, if two thirds of all the state legislatures request it, Congress must call a convention to propose amendments. All proposed amendments must be ratified by three quarters of the states to go into effect.

Each house of Congress can also review the qualifications of its members. For example, if a person has been elected to the Senate in an improper way, the Senate may refuse to admit the person. Each house may also expel a member for misconduct.

Congress is also responsible for settling any disputes in national elections. In 1876, when Rutherford B. Hayes and Samuel J. Tilden were the two main presidential candidates, there were two sets of electoral votes from four states and no clear winner. Congress appointed a special commission to decide which votes to accept. In the end, Hayes was declared the winner by one electoral vote.

If no candidate for president receives a majority of electoral votes, the election is decided by the House of Representatives. In this case, voting in the House is by state. Only in two elections—Thomas Jefferson's in 1800, and John Quincy Adams's in 1824—has the House had to choose the president.

Finally, if no candidate for vice president has a majority of electoral votes, the Senate makes the decision. This has not yet happened.

C H A P T E R

4

HOW CONGRESS WORKS

Since 1789, every Congress has been given a number.
In 1789, the First Congress met. The Congress that
began in 1993 was the 103d Congress.

Every Congress lasts for two years. The first year
of a new Congress is called that Congress's first
session. The second year is called the second session.

During each session, laws are proposed, written,
and voted upon. Most proposals, or bills, must be
voted upon and passed within a limited time frame.
Many bills have "died" because they did not come
up for a vote before Congress adjourned (ended) its
session. So how does a bill successfully become a
law? It is a long procedure, but it is a process that
makes sure that all views have been expressed.

Opposite:
**Speaker of the
House Thomas
Foley (behind
podium) speaks
about budget issues
at a press
conference.**

Congress Starts Work on a Law

Any person may have an idea for a law. But to become a federal law, that idea must first be introduced in Congress by one or more members. When a law is proposed in Congress, it is called a bill.

Most bills may be introduced in either house of Congress or in both houses at the same time. The exception is a bill to raise money, like a proposal for a new tax. The Constitution requires that such a law be introduced in the House of Representatives. This requirement comes from the principle of "no taxation without representation." The idea is that members of the House, who are elected every two years, most closely represent the people of our nation. By custom, any appropriation bills (bills that propose how the government's money will be spent) must also start in the House.

Each house of Congress works separately on bills. Each may change or "kill" a bill as it sees fit.

While members of Congress look on, Vice President Al Gore talks to the press about a bill in February 1993.

The Committee System

After a bill is introduced, the leadership—the Speaker of the House and the majority leader in the Senate—assigns it to the appropriate committee or committees. The committees of Congress are essential to its work. Without them, the House and Senate would work much more slowly because they could handle only one matter at a time.

As of 1993, the House had twenty-two and the Senate had sixteen standing, or permanent, committees. Within each house, every standing committee has a particular responsibility: agriculture, appropriations, armed services, finance (called "ways and means" in the House of Representatives), foreign affairs, labor, and several others. In the House, a standing committee may have from twenty to fifty members; in the Senate, ten to twenty members is the

The Senate Ethics
Committee, which
currently has six
members, hears
testimony in
November 1990.

average. Committees are then further divided into subcommittees. Committees and subcommittees are led by chairmen or chairwomen, who always belong to the majority party.

A committee studies a bill. It may hold hearings and question experts on the issue concerned. Then the committee decides whether to recommend the bill, with or without changes, to the full House or Senate. If the committee decides against recommending the bill, it is very unlikely that the bill will become law.

In the Senate, the Family and Medical Leave bill was assigned to the Labor Committee. Hearings were held in January 1991 by a subcommittee, and in April the committee approved the bill. In the House, the bill came before the Education and Labor Committee and the Post Office Committee (because postal workers were covered by it). In addition, a subcommittee of the Education and Labor Committee held hearings in February 1991. Both House committees approved the bill in March.

Committees do not work only on bills. In fact, virtually *all* of Congress's business goes to one or more committees. For example, when the president nominates a person to the Supreme Court, the nomination is considered first by the Senate Judiciary Committee. Similarly, a proposed treaty is first looked at by the Senate Foreign Relations Committee.

Occasionally, a select committee is created for a specific purpose. Examples include the House and Senate committees that were created to investigate the Watergate scandal in 1974. There are also several joint committees composed of members from both houses. These committees, like the Joint Economic Committee, study particular subjects. Select and joint committees do not usually work on bills.

Debate, Voting, and Passage

Once a bill has been approved by the appropriate committee, it goes to the full House or Senate for debate and voting. In the House, the bill must also pass through the Rules Committee. The Rules Committee sets guidelines for the House's debate on the bill. In the Senate, the leadership places the bill on the calendar.

Since the House has 435 members, each representative usually has only a few minutes to speak on each issue that is being considered. In the 100-member Senate, there is unlimited time for debate.

During the debates that take place in each house, representatives and senators make speeches for or against the bill. Some may make suggestions for amending it. When the debate is concluded, the vote on the bill takes place. To speed things up, the House now has a method of recording votes electronically.

House and Senate debates and votes can be watched on the cable television station C-SPAN. You can also read the written records of debates in the *Congressional Record,* which is printed every day that Congress meets.

To pass Congress, a bill must be approved by a majority of those voting in each house. Often a bill is approved in differing forms by the two houses. When that happens, the bill goes to a conference committee. A conference committee is a temporary committee of people from both houses who are appointed by the congressional leadership. Its purpose is to work out a single version of the bill. The conference committee then reports back to each house, which must approve the committee's version by majority vote.

A FILIBUSTER

Senators have the privilege during debate of talking for as long as they wish. Occasionally, the privilege is used to prevent action on a measure that would otherwise be approved. The procedure, called a filibuster, works like this: One or more senators may strongly oppose a bill or nomination that they do not have enough votes to defeat. So they continue to talk until the Senate agrees to drop or postpone the matter.

The longest filibuster on record was by Senator Strom Thurmond of South Carolina. In 1957, Senator Thurmond tried to filibuster a civil rights bill to death. He spoke continuously for twenty-four hours and eighteen minutes! (The bill eventually passed anyway.)

A filibuster can be broken only if sixty senators—three fifths of the entire Senate—vote to terminate the debate. Such a vote, which is called cloture, is difficult to obtain.

The full Senate debated the Family and Medical Leave bill and passed it, after making some changes, by a vote of 65 to 32 on October 2, 1991. The House passed it, with changes, by 287 to 143 on November 13, 1991. Since there were some differences between the Senate and the House versions, the bill had to go to a conference committee. But not until August 1992, did the conference committee meet and work out the differences. The Senate approved the committee's version on August 11, and the House approved it on September 10.

The Proposed Law Goes to the President

If each house passes the conference committee's version of the bill, the bill then goes to the president for signing. The president has ten days (not counting Sundays) to consider the bill. If the president signs it, the bill becomes a law. But the president may veto, or reject, the bill. A vetoed bill is sent back to Congress. Unless two thirds of each house votes to override the president's veto, the bill cannot become a law. If the president vetoes a bill and the particular Congress that passed it has permanently adjourned, or ended, before the ten days are up, the veto cannot be overridden. This procedure is called a pocket veto.

The presidential veto and Congress's ability to override the veto are further examples of the checks and balances system that is built into the Constitution.

President George Bush had been against the Family and Medical Leave bill all along. On September 22, 1992, he vetoed the bill, saying it was wrong for the government to tell businesses what they must do.

Congressional backers of the bill then tried to have the House and the Senate override President Bush's veto. The Senate voted 68 to 31 for the bill, and had 2 votes more than the two-thirds majority that was needed to override. But the House failed to override the veto. It voted for the bill 258 to 169, but was 27 votes short of the needed two-thirds majority. The bill was then considered dead.

However, the story did not end there. Shortly after the new 103d Congress met in January 1993, a new president, Bill Clinton, took office. Clinton had expressed strong support for the family and medical leave idea during his election campaign. Several members of the new Congress decided to try again. They promptly introduced a bill that was very similar to the one Bush had vetoed. Both houses acted swiftly. Within a few weeks, the bill had cleared the appropriate committees in both houses. The House of Representatives and the Senate passed the same bill on February 4. President Clinton signed it on February 5. The bill was now law as the Family and Medical Leave Act of 1993.

Opposite: **President Clinton signs the Family and Medical Leave bill while Vicki Yandle and members of Congress look on. Yandle, who lost her job when she took time off to take care of her ill child, is typical of the people this bill is intended to protect.**

TEMPERS IN CONGRESS

Members of Congress are usually very polite to one another. In their speeches, they may refer to each other as "my good friend" or "my distinguished colleague."

But there have been exceptions. In the years just before the Civil War, the slavery issue caused tempers to flare. Probably the worst incident in Congress occurred in May 1856.

Senator Charles Sumner of Massachusetts was bitterly opposed to slavery. While expressing his views during a debate, he made many vicious remarks about several fellow senators. One was Andrew Butler of South Carolina. Butler was absent at the time, but two days later, Butler's nephew, Congressman Preston Brooks, walked into the Senate. Sumner was sitting at his desk. Brooks beat him with a cane so badly that Sumner was left bleeding and unconscious.

Brooks resigned two months later but was eventually unanimously re-elected.

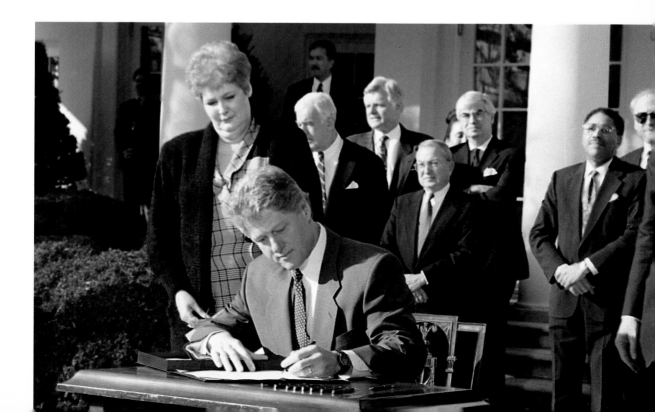

5

INFLUENCING CONGRESS

Because what Congress does is so important to the lives of all Americans (and even to people in other countries), many people try to influence its actions.

Government Officials

On many occasions during their terms of office, presidents make speeches to Congress—and sometimes directly to the American people—urging Congress to take certain actions.

Other government officials also ask Congress to act. Often they come and talk to Congressional committees. Heads of executive branch departments make reports to Congress. The secretary of defense may ask for certain military bases to be closed, or for money to build a new weapons system. The secretary

Opposite:
President Bill Clinton waves to the crowd on February 17, 1993, before addressing a joint session of Congress about his economic plans. Vice President Al Gore (left) and House Speaker Thomas Foley (right) applaud the president.

41

President George Bush (center) greets a joint session of Congress in September 1990.

The Constitution states that the president "shall from time to time give to the Congress Information of the State of the Union, and recommend to their Consideration such Measures as he shall judge necessary and expedient."

Accordingly, early each year, the president makes a speech to Congress called the State of the Union Address. In his speech, the president discusses what he feels are the most urgent issues facing the country and makes recommendations about actions he thinks Congress should take. Many of his recommendations become the subjects of bills that Congress considers.

The president may also address Congress on issues of great importance. For example, in September 1993, President Clinton addressed Congress about health care.

When the president addresses Congress, the members of the House and Senate assemble together in what is called a joint session. They meet in the hall of the House of Representatives, since it is larger than the Senate chamber, to hear the president speak.

of housing and urban development may suggest a program to build low-cost housing. The secretary of the treasury may ask for changes in the tax laws.

The director of the Federal Bureau of Investigation (FBI) regularly reports on crime in America and how to reduce it. The Surgeon General may urge Congress to require stronger warnings on cigarette packs about the dangers of smoking. These are just a few examples.

It's not only federal officials who try to influence Congress. State, county, and city governments are also very concerned with what Congress does. Many local governments maintain offices in Washington so they can keep closely in touch with what is going on. Officials from large cities, for example, try to persuade Congress to provide more money for transportation.

Special Interest Groups

A special interest group is a group of people that seeks to influence government policies. There are many different interest groups. Business people, consumers, farmers, workers, and teachers have all formed organizations in order to promote their views. So have people concerned about the environment, civil rights, women's issues, and other subjects.

Interest groups want to know how government policies will affect them. For example, the Family and Medical Leave bill aroused the concern of several interest groups. Women's rights organizations and labor unions that represented workers supported the bill. Some organizations that represented businesses opposed it. These groups all made their views known to the members of Congress.

Representative Pat Schroeder talks to representatives of women's organizations who wanted the Family and Medical Leave bill passed in 1992.

Such efforts are called lobbying. Interest group representatives are known as lobbyists, since they wait in lobbies outside offices in order to talk to members of Congress. There are thousands of lobbyists in Washington, D.C.

Lobbying is a very important activity. By lobbying, interest groups make it clear how they want Congress to vote. At the same time, members of

HOW TO WRITE TO MEMBERS OF CONGRESS

Members of Congress want to hear from the people in their home districts or states. They want to know what *you* think. When you feel strongly about an issue in the news, write and tell your representative or senators what you think about it.

Here are some tips for writing an effective letter:

1. Identify yourself—say how old you are and what school you attend.

2. Clearly state your purpose at the beginning of your letter and keep the letter short and to the point.

3. Sign your letter and be sure to include your return address so your representative or senator can reply to you.

4. If you hand-write your letter, be sure it is legible!

The address for a member of the United States House of Representatives is:

The Honorable [full name of the representative]
United States House of Representatives
Washington, DC 20515

The address for a member of the United States Senate is:

The Honorable [full name of the senator]
United States Senate
Washington, DC 20510

Congress often rely on lobbyists for information about how people feel and will be affected by proposals.

Interest groups do more than present their views. They may endorse candidates for election to Congress and contribute money to the candidates' campaigns. Many groups have formed what are called political action committees (PACs) just for that purpose.

Of course, it is illegal for members of Congress (or other government officials) to ask for, or accept, money or gifts in return for acting in a certain way. Congress also has its own rules concerning relations with lobbyists.

The Voters

Members of Congress are interested not only in what the president, other government officials, and interest groups have to say. They also care very much about the opinions of average citizens. After all, it is the people who elect representatives and senators.

For this reason, members of Congress pay close attention to what their constituents (voters in their home states) think. They watch public opinion polls carefully. They maintain offices in their home communities and make frequent trips home to keep in touch. Members of Congress send out questionnaires asking people's views on the leading issues of the day. They also take the mail they receive from their constituents very seriously.

The U.S. Congress represents the people of the United States. The voice of the people counts!

Chronology

1765	Stamp Act Congress protests "taxation without representation."
1774	First Continental Congress asserts colonial rights against Britain.
1775	Second Continental Congress appoints George Washington commander of American army.
1776	Second Continental Congress declares America independent of Britain.
1781	Articles of Confederation ratified.
1787	Constitutional Convention creates new government for United States.
1789	Constitution goes into effect; First United States Congress meets; Washington becomes president.
1800	House of Representatives elects Jefferson president.
1824	House of Representatives elects John Quincy Adams president.
1868	Congress impeaches but narrowly fails to convict President Andrew Johnson.
1876	Congressional commission rules Rutherford B. Hayes winner of presidential election.
1911	Congress sets 435 members as size of House of Representatives.
1913	Seventeenth Amendment provides for direct election of U.S. senators by the people.
1974	Congress holds special hearings to investigate the Watergate scandal. President Nixon resigns to avoid impeachment.
1990s	Congress debates national health care reform and considers one of the most sweeping changes in the twentieth century. More women, African Americans, and other minorities take office than ever before.

For Further Reading

Bernstein, Richard, and Jerome Agel. *Congress.* New York: Walker & Co., 1989.

Green, Carl, and William Sanford. *Congress.* Vero Beach, FL: Rourke, 1990.

Johnson, Linda Carlson. *Our Constitution.* Brookfield, CT: The Millbrook Press, 1992.

Schlesinger, Arthur M., ed. *The Federal Government: How It Works.* Broomall, PA: Chelsea House, 1990.

Stein, R. C. *The Powers of Congress.* Chicago: Childrens Press, 1989.

Index